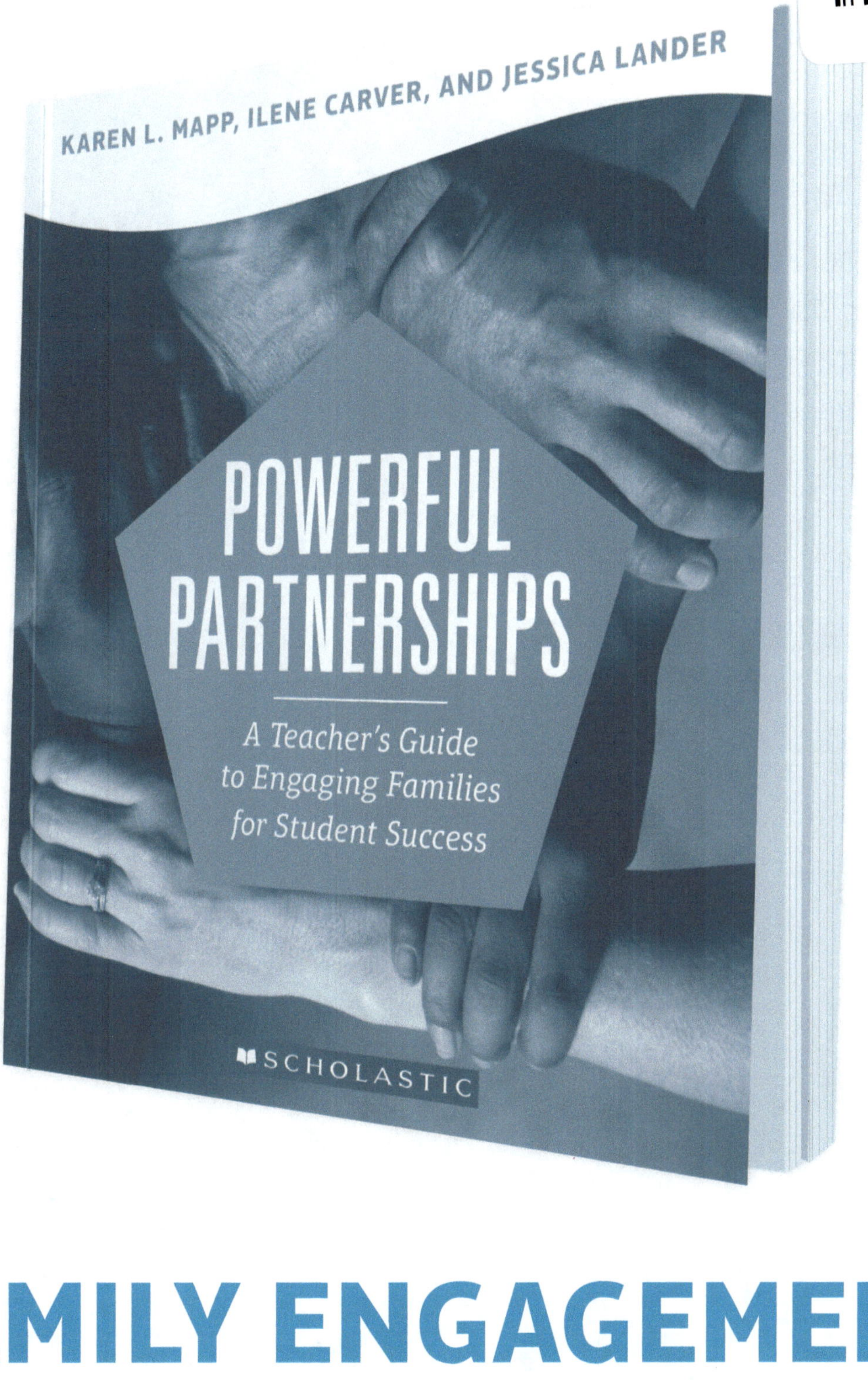
KAREN L. MAPP, ILENE CARVER, AND JESSICA LANDER
POWERFUL PARTNERSHIPS
A Teacher's Guide to Engaging Families for Student Success
SCHOLASTIC

FAMILY ENGAGEMENT
ACTION GUIDE

SCHOLASTIC

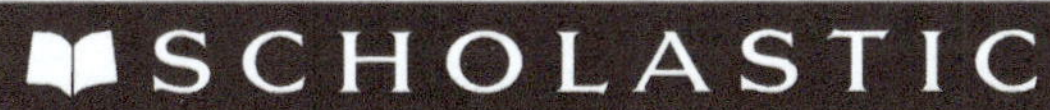

TABLE OF CONTENTS

ACKNOWLEDGMENTS

Scholastic would like to acknowledge the collaboration of our pilot Book Study group, led by Dr. Judy Carson, the Program Manager for School-Family-Community Partnerships at the Connecticut State Department of Education and Jessie B. Lavorgna, the Family, School & Community Partnership Specialist at the Education Development Center. We also gratefully acknowledge the book study participants: Kimberly Bobin, Nicole Michna Bradeen, Peggy Cormeny, Nitza Diaz, Dawn Dubay, Eric Galm, Yolanta Garcia, Shelly Garow, Michael Gonzales, Svetlana Grishtaev, Patricia Jomo, Donna Koser, Mary Beth Kuzoian, Beverly Lawrence, Betsy Leborious, Jill Mahoney, Donna Marino, Veronica Marion, Michelle McKnight, Nancy Mendez, Ashley Monier, Sonya Montoya, Christina Morales, Sheryle Perkins, Shelby Pons, Kelly Rall, Teresa Rodriguez, Terri Scott, Camille Smith, Anne Tranquilli-Bausher, Deborah Watson, Joanne White, Renee Wiley, Sebrina Wilson, Amy Yarbrough, and Cynthia Zingler.

ISBN-13: 978-1-338-56483-9 ISBN-10: 1-338-56483-8

Scholastic is constantly working to lessen the environmental impact of our manufacturing processes. To view our industry-leading paper procurement policy, visit www.scholastic.com/paperpolicy.

2 3 4 5 6 7 8 9 10 150 28 27 26 25 24 23

Text pages printed on 10% PCW recycled paper.

Scholastic Inc., 557 Broadway, New York, NY 10012

A Note from Karen Mapp

Meaningful partnerships between families and schools are essential to student success. When families are involved in their children's education, the benefits are widespread and too numerous to count.

In 2017, Ilene Carver, Jessica Lander, and I published *Powerful Partnerships: A Teacher's Guide to Engaging Families for Student Success.* We designed the book with one goal in mind: to encourage teachers to see family engagement as a fundamental and achievable component of their instructional practice.

We recognize that most teachers have had little opportunity in their pre-service training to receive strong guidance in this area. *Powerful Partnerships* was written for you, the teacher, to provide you with the tools you need to partner effectively with families.

Our hope is that this companion study guide will help you and your colleagues put those best practices into action, and take family engagement to a deeper level. We designed this guide as a professional learning opportunity to help foster conversation among you and your peers around the most essential elements of effective family engagement.

The guide follows *Powerful Partnerships* chapter-by-chapter, with suggestions for group facilitators and online tips if you choose to have virtual meetings. However you choose to structure your study, the guide will foster important conversations to gain the most from reading the book. It will help you to confront any obstacles within yourself, and provide you the tools to begin planning for partnership.

You can create powerful partnerships with every one of your families. We have designed this guide and *Powerful Partnerships* to help you take the next step.

WEEK ONE

Introduction: Build Your Case for Family Engagement

REFLECT, JOT & DISCUSS:

Use the space provided to reflect on each question and jot your own ideas. If you have the opportunity, you may then discuss and share your thoughts with each other.

TIP FOR FACILITATORS

- Send a welcome email and remind participants of the discussion expectations before meeting. For example: What chapter(s) should be read? Are any materials needed?
- Consider distributing a survey to assess participants' background knowledge, as well as their hopes for the book study, and use the results to help guide your future discussions.
- If this book study guide has already been distributed, encourage everyone to skim through the first chapter before you meet to get an idea of what the discussion will entail. If not, it may be helpful to share a few questions in advance to jump-start their thinking!

1 The introduction begins by touching on four situations that bring teachers a sense of well-being and accomplishment. How do you personally measure success? Can it be found within the four ideas bulleted in this chapter? Or do you measure success differently, and if so, how?

____

____

____

____

____

____

____

2 Page 5 acknowledges that a variety of factors contribute to an educator's success. Place the success factors on the continuum below to indicate how much of an impact you believe they have on your own success. You may also add your own key contributors if you feel any are missing. Be ready to share the factor that affects your success the most and why it has this impact.

Success Factors

- Competent, positive leader(s)
- Instructional guidance and support
- Skilled coworkers
- Strong community ties
- Strong family ties
- ______________
- ______________
- ______________

NO IMPACT ⟷ LARGE IMPACT

3 According to pages 5 and 6, research shows that family partnerships yield the following results:

- Children's grades go up.
- Children attend school more regularly.
- Children are more likely to enroll in higher-level programs.
- Children are more likely to graduate and go on to college.
- Children are more excited and positive about school and learning.
- Children have fewer discipline problems inside and outside the classroom.

Do any of your personal experiences align with this research? How? If not, do you believe family engagement has the potential to have this impact? Why or why not?

TIP FOR VIRTUAL GROUPS

Just as you would with an in-person meeting, begin with an introduction where participants share their names, roles, and what they hope to gain from this book study. Building a sense of community is equally important in a virtual environment. Zoom and Facebook Live are two platforms you can explore for virtual meetings.

As a teacher and administrator, I have witnessed students having more investment in education when families are involved. But the question that weighs on me is: How do we create longer-term investment for parents (not just one-and-done involvement), so that the results are even deeper? And, how do we reach the parents who do not feel welcome or don't have an investment?

—NICOLE BRADEEN, Senior Associate, Great Schools Partnership, Inc.

4 Throughout this book, you will read teachers' personal reflections on family engagement in their classrooms. You will also often be asked to personally reflect on your own relationships with students' families. For your first reflection, think broadly and fill in the chart below.

Examples of Positive Family Relationships (What made them positive?)	Examples of Difficult Family Relationships (What made them difficult?)

As you share these relationships, consider: What similarities can you find in the positive experiences? What may have helped the difficult relationships become more positive?

LOOKING AHEAD:

1 Pages 12 and 13 provide a brief overview of the rest of the book. Take a few moments to record your initial reactions to the upcoming chapters. Then share: Which chapter(s) has the potential to make the most impact on your teaching practice? Why? Are there any chapters that you feel apprehensive or unsure about exploring? Why?

2 Reread the Final Thoughts section at the very end of the introduction and watch the "Introduction: Your Colleagues Reflect" video available at scholastic.com/pro/PartnershipsResources.html if you haven't already. Then answer the question below.

Think about a time when you partnered with a family to support a student in your own classroom and the impact it had on the child, on the family, and on your teaching. Then consider: What aspects of family engagement in your classroom do you hope to grow and improve?

Try to take the time to share your individual goals with one another. Being aware of how your colleagues hope to grow and what they hope to get out of the next several weeks is an important step in building a relationship with each other!

Chapter 1: Examine Your Core Beliefs

REFLECT, JOT & DISCUSS:

Use the space provided to reflect on each question and jot your own ideas. If you have the opportunity, you may then discuss and share your thoughts with each other.

1 Chapter One begins with a discussion of core beliefs: the idea that every decision we make ties back to our personal values. Core beliefs affect not only who we are as individuals, but who we are as educators as well. Each and every action we take in our classroom and our school community is rooted in our core beliefs. For this reason, we'll begin by examining them.

Reflecting on core beliefs is not easy. Our core beliefs may stem from experiences that we don't often think about, and they're incredibly personal in nature. To help you begin to think about your own core beliefs, use the chart below to work through the questions that are presented at the beginning of Chapter 1. Don't worry about sharing your responses with the group. This is for you. If you need more room, please continue on a separate piece of paper.

A REFLECTION ON MY CORE BELIEFS			
School Experience: How was your family connected or not connected to your school and educational experience?	**Shaping Beliefs:** How might these past experiences, positive or negative, shape your beliefs as a teacher about family engagement?	**Barriers:** What fears, hesitations, or apprehensions do you have about this work? What barriers will you have to overcome?	**Commitments:** What passions, beliefs, and commitments do you bring that will help you do this work?

- Encourage participants to complete Question 1 before meeting. Core beliefs are personal and often difficult to reflect upon, so it's important that everyone has the chance to complete this independently.
- If possible, prepare for a discussion of Question 2 by displaying four pieces of chart paper, each labeled with one of Dr. Mapp's essential core beliefs. A gallery walk (in which participants move from paper to paper, review the ideas of others, and then add their own thoughts) may be a productive discussion structure for this multifaceted question.

2 Now that you've begun to consider your own core beliefs, let's think about the four essential core beliefs that are presented beginning on page 19. These core beliefs are called "essential" because Dr. Mapp believes all teachers must truly believe in them in order to achieve successful family engagement. The reflection prompts on the next page restate each of the core beliefs and then provide you with guiding questions meant to help you contemplate each belief more thoroughly. Be ready to share your responses!

Before each session, send out 1–3 reflection questions that participants may benefit from thinking about in advance. It can be more difficult to facilitate introspective reflection when you are meeting virtually, and sending reflection questions beforehand gives participants the opportunity to do this in their own time leading up to the discussion.

People need to know you truly care before they will open up, especially when they have had a bad experience in the past. Being authentic, honest, and understanding makes a great start to a partnership.

—JILL MAHONEY, Executive Director, CT Partnership for Children

CORE BELIEF #1: All families have dreams for their children and want the best for them.

a. Is there a time that sticks out in your mind related to this core belief?

b. I do/don't struggle with this belief because:

c. Based on your reading, what could you consider if/when you struggle?

CORE BELIEF #2: All families have the capacity to support their children's learning.

a. The time I may have been most surprised to see this to be true was:

b. Turn to page 23 and reread strengths #1–8. Are you making the most of the strengths and assets your families have to offer? Why or why not?

c. Page 25 explains that strength-based thinkers look at the world with the belief that everyone has their own unique tool kit. How could you enhance the way you utilize the strengths, the tools, and the assets of your families?

CORE BELIEF #3: Families and school staff are equal partners.

a. What does it mean to be equal partners? Does equal mean "the same"? Why or why not?

____

____

____

b. What do you already value about the families you work with?

____

____

____

c. What can you do to further show families that they are valued and respected?

____

____

____

If we can show families that we care about their communities in a sustained and meaningful way, then the trust begins to be built and communication can start.

—SONYA MONTOYA, Family Services Manager, Northern Arizona Council of Governments Head Start

CORE BELIEF #4: The responsibility for cultivating and sustaining partnerships among school, home, and community rests primarily with school staff, especially school leaders.

a. The research brief on pages 29–31 discusses the need for parents to trust their school before they become active participants. What could you or your school do to promote trust and start more authentic lines of communication between parents and staff members?

To promote trust, my school could:	To promote trust, I could:

b. Watch the accompanying Chapter 1 video at scholastic.com/pro/PartnershipsResources.html in which educators share their own engagement strategies. Feel free to add new ideas to your chart as you discuss, watch, and listen!

LOOKING BACK in order to LOOK AHEAD:

1 Page 33 quotes author Beverly Tatum: "I assume that we all have prejudices, not because we want them, but simply because we are so continually exposed to misinformation about others." The chapter then goes on to discuss the existence of prejudices in everyone's lives. In particular, it urges us as educators to take the time to examine the role race plays in our own core beliefs in order for us to strengthen our relationships with families.

Take some time to consider the words above and then reflect on an experience where race, class, language, or another difference made your relationship with a student's family more difficult. Which essential core belief could you have embraced more heavily in order to build a more successful relationship? How?

---

2 How can continuing to be more aware of this core belief help guide your family relationships over the next school year?

Be prepared to share these closing reflections and goals. Despite the vast differences that make each of your family relationships unique, you may be surprised at how alike they can be too!

Chapter 2: Harness the Power of Partnerships

REFLECT, JOT & DISCUSS:

Use the space provided to reflect on each question and jot your own ideas. If you have the opportunity, you may then discuss and share your thoughts with each other.

1 As Chapter 2 acknowledges, everyone has hopefully been fortunate enough to be in a successful partnership at some point in their lives, whether it involved a friend, significant other, colleague or sibling. Let's follow the book's suggestion and begin by thinking about this particular partnership. Why was it successful? What did you enjoy about it? How exactly did you collaborate, and why did you complement each other? Jot down a description of the partnership below and be ready to share why and how it worked.

2a Now that you have a model of a positive partnership in mind, let's reflect on family partnerships within your school. Page 38 mentions a partnership rubric in another book by Dr. Mapp and her colleagues called *Beyond the Bake Sale: The Essential Guide to Family-School Partnerships*. A copy of this rubric is shown on the following pages. Please follow the directions on the rubric and complete it thoughtfully, without worry about judgments or implications, and then return to 2b on the following pages.

TIP FOR FACILITATORS

- If participants have indicated that they have time to reflect on questions before meeting, Questions 1, 2a, and 2b would benefit from independent reflection. Completion of these questions in advance means that participants can come already able to share where their school falls on the Four Versions of Family-School Partnerships rubric.
- Two videos are included in this week's reflection. If a projector is not available for your session, email the video links just prior to the discussion so participants can watch the videos on their mobile devices during the book study.

Four Versions of Family-School Partnership

Check the boxes with the most bulleted statements that apply to your school. Check only one box in each row.

PARTNERSHIP SCHOOL	OPEN-DOOR SCHOOL	COME-IF-WE-CALL SCHOOL	FORTRESS SCHOOL
All families & communities have something great to offer—we do whatever it takes to work closely together to make sure every single student succeeds.	Parents can be involved at our school in many ways—we're working hard to get an even bigger turnout for our activities. When we ask the community to help, people often respond.	Parents are welcome when we ask them, but there's only so much they can offer. The most important thing they can do is help their kids at home. We know where to get community help if we need it.	Parents belong at home, not at school. If students don't do well, it's because their families don't give them enough support. We're already doing all we can. Our school is an oasis in a troubled community. We want to keep it that way.
☐ **Building Relationships** • Family center is always open, full of interesting learning materials to borrow • Home visits are made to every new family • Activities honor families' contributions • Building is open to community use and social services are available to families	☐ **Building Relationships** • Teachers contact families once a year • Parent coordinator is available if families have questions or need help • Office staff are friendly • Staff contact community agencies and organizations when help is needed	☐ **Building Relationships** • Better-educated parents are more involved • "Many immigrant parents don't have time to come or contribute" • Staff are very selective about who comes into the school	☐ **Building Relationships** • Families do not "bother" school staff • "Minority families don't value education" • Parents need security clearance to come in • It is important to keep community influences out of the school
☐ **Linking to Learning** • All family activities connect to what students are learning • Parents and teachers look at student work and test results together • Community groups offer tutoring and homework programs at the school • Students' work goes home every week with a scoring guide	☐ **Linking to Learning** • Teachers explain test scores if asked • Folders of student work go home occasionally • School holds curriculum nights three or four times a year • Staff let families know about out-of-school classes in the community	☐ **Linking to Learning** • Parents are told what students will be learning at the fall open house • Parents can call the office to get teacher-recorded messages about homework • Workshops are offered on parenting	☐ **Linking to Learning** • Curriculum and standards are considered too complex for parents to understand • "If parents want more information, they can ask for it" • "We're teachers, not social workers"
☐ **Addressing Differences** • Translators are readily available • Teachers use books and materials about families' cultures • PTA includes all families • Local groups help staff reach parents	☐ **Addressing Differences** • Office staff will find a translator if parents ask in advance • Multicultural nights are held once a year • "Minority" parents have their own group	☐ **Addressing Differences** • "We can't deal with twenty different languages" • "Parents can bring a translator with them" • "This school just isn't the same as it used to be"	☐ **Addressing Differences** • "Those parents need to learn English" • "We teach about our country—that's what those parents need to know" • "This neighborhood is going downhill"
☐ **Supporting Advocacy** • There is a clear, open process for resolving problems • Teachers contact families each month to discuss student progress • Student-led parent-teacher conferences are held three times a year for thirty minutes	☐ **Supporting Advocacy** • Principal will meet with parents to discuss a problem • Regular progress reports go to parents, but test data can be hard to understand • Parent-teacher conferences are held twice a year	☐ **Supporting Advocacy** • School calls families when children have problems • Families visit school on report card pickup day and can see a teacher if they call first	☐ **Supporting Advocacy** • Parents don't come to conferences • Problems are dealt with by the professional staff • Teachers don't feel safe with parents
☐ **Sharing Power** • Parents and teachers research issues such as prejudice and tracking • Parent group is focused on improving student achievement • Families are involved in all major decisions • Parents can use the school's phone, copier, fax, and computers • Staff work with local organizations to improve the school and neighborhood	☐ **Sharing Power** • Parents can raise issues at PTA meetings or see the principal • Parent group sets its own agenda and raises money for the school • Resource center for low-income families is housed in a portable classroom next to the school • PTA officers can use the school office • A community representative sits on the school council	☐ **Sharing Power** • Principal sets agenda for parent meetings • PTA gets the school's message out • "Parents are not experts in education" • Community groups can address the school board if they have concerns	☐ **Sharing Power** • Principal picks a small group of "cooperative parents" to help out • Families are afraid to complain: "They might take it out on my kid" • "Community groups should mind their own business; they don't know about education"

2b Now that you have finished the rubric, score yourself using the directions below:

- If three or more of your checked boxes fall in the Fortress School section and none fall under Open-Door or Partnership, your school is trying to keep parents away rather than work with them. In standards-based terms, it is below basic.
- If three or more of your checked boxes fall under Come-If-We-Call and none are under Partnership, your school may want parents to be involved only on its terms. In standards-based terms, it is at the basic level.
- If at least four of your checked boxes fall under Open-Door or Partnership and none are under Fortress School, your school welcomes families and supports them to be involved in a number of ways. In standards-based terms, it is proficient.
- If at least three of your checked boxes are under Partnership and the rest are under Open-Door, your school is willing and able to work with all families. We bet the student achievement level goes up every year. In standards-based terms, it is advanced.

Examine your results and consider: Does any part of it surprise you? Why?

____

____

____

Don't let yourself be overwhelmed by your school's score. The important part is that you now have a starting point for partnerships in your school and classroom as you move forward!

3a On page 43, you read that Dr. Mapp collaborated with the U.S. Department of Education (USDOE) to create the USDOE Dual Capacity Framework for Family-School Partnership. This was created to provide a tangible resource that schools and educators could use to help engage in meaningful family partnerships. Before you move on, take a moment to review the framework at http://www.sedl.org/pubs/framework/ and then listen to "Understanding the Dual Capacity-Building Framework," an explanation of the theory behind it, under the Video Links section at www.scholastic.com/pro/PartnershipsResources.html. If you have any overarching questions, jot them here in case you have time to discuss them with your group:

____

____

____

____

3b

As a teacher, you have the most control over the Opportunity Condition block of this framework. Page 43 states that there are five process conditions that need to be built into the planning of a family engagement event, program, or initiative to ensure its success. Follow the instructions included in the chart below to help you think through each of these conditions. Once the chart is complete, try to share your responses and take this opportunity to learn from your peers.

PROCESS CONDITION For further information refer to pages 43–46.	**Example(s) of personal success with each process condition** If you're unsure, you may jot an example that someone shares.	**How could I (better) achieve this?** Reread page 46 to refresh your memory on how adults learn best. Then use these to think of actionable ways you could be more successful.	**Which school stakeholders (if any) could I ask for support from in order to be more successful?** You can't do everything alone!
LINKED TO LEARNING: Do my families leave the events in my classroom knowing more about what their children should know and be able to do?			
RELATIONAL: Do families and school staff have an opportunity to learn about each other, to share stories, and to build partnerships that are based on respect?			
DEVELOPMENTAL: Do you assume that families already have strengths and knowledge on which you can build?			
COLLABORATIVE: Do you strive to bring families and staff (yourself included) together so that they can learn from and with each other?			
INTERACTIVE: Do you provide families with an opportunity to practice and discuss the activities that you'd like them to complete with their children at home?			

LOOKING BACK in order to LOOK AHEAD:

1 Watch the Chapter 2 Colleague Reflection video at www.scholastic.com/pro/PartnershipsResources.html. Then consider what these educators expressed and fill in the sentence starters below. Be ready to share the sentence that is most meaningful to you.

One connection I have is: ______________________________

____

____

One statement that surprised me was: ______________________________

____

____

because ______________________________

Something I heard that I would like to keep in mind moving forward is: ______________________________

____

____

One idea someone shared that I would like to commit to trying is: ______________________________

____

____

because ______________________________

2 Over the course of studying this chapter, you assessed where your school currently falls on the Four Versions of Family-School Partnerships rubric. You evaluated your process condition successes, and you pinpointed areas where you could improve. You also listened to colleagues (those in the video and/or those in your discussion group) articulate their successes and struggles.

Out of all the information you're now processing, what is the single biggest takeaway you would like to remember as you move forward?

____

____

____

____

____

It's key to remember that communication means talking "with" and not "to" others. Being able to seek feedback and digest it is as important as being able to effectively deliver it.

—PATRICIA JOMO, Freelancer in Family Engagement in Education, Greenwich Public Schools

TIP FOR VIRTUAL GROUPS

Now that a few sessions are complete, consider how your virtual discussion platform is working. Are group members able to easily share? Is there a way for interested participants to look back on each session? If your initial format is not working as well as it could be, don't be afraid to switch!

Chapter 3: Welcome, Honor, and Connect with Your Families

REFLECT, JOT & DISCUSS:

Use the space provided to reflect on each question and jot your own ideas. If you have the opportunity, you may then discuss and share your thoughts with each other.

1a This chapter focuses primarily on first impressions. Think about a time in your life when you had a positive first impression as well as a negative first impression, and record what happened side by side below. What factors contributed to these impressions?

Positive First Impression	Negative First Impression

TIP FOR FACILITATORS

Encourage participants to complete Questions 1 and 2 before meeting as a group. All participants should take a moment to look back through their plan book, their first week of school folder, or wherever they keep track of their back-to-school to-do list before they complete Question 2. It can be easy to forget the little things we do at the beginning of the school year to welcome students and families—but these little things are often what have the biggest impact!

1b Upon thinking about your impressions above, and perhaps even listening to the first impressions of your peers, what seem to be some of the key characteristics that distinguish a positive first impression from a negative first impression?

2 Now think about your own classroom. How do you normally welcome families to the start of a new school year? What kind of impression do you think this gives? Why?

3 This chapter discusses the three key components to what Dr. Mapp calls the Joining Process: Welcoming, Honoring, and Connecting. In particular, it focuses on three foundational strategies for building an effective family-school partnership early on. Below, we'll dive into each of these strategies.

Foundational Strategy 1: Welcome Phone Calls

Your first contact with a family sets a lasting tone for the duration of the year—and has the power to welcome families and encourage them to engage with you! Pages 53–54 provide tips for what you could include in your call, but what you say is really up to you.

Below is space to create a model script that could be used during your welcome phone calls this coming school year. You may choose to leave the family lines blank and instead map out what you want to make sure to say. If given the opportunity, find a colleague with whom you can role-play this script once it is complete!

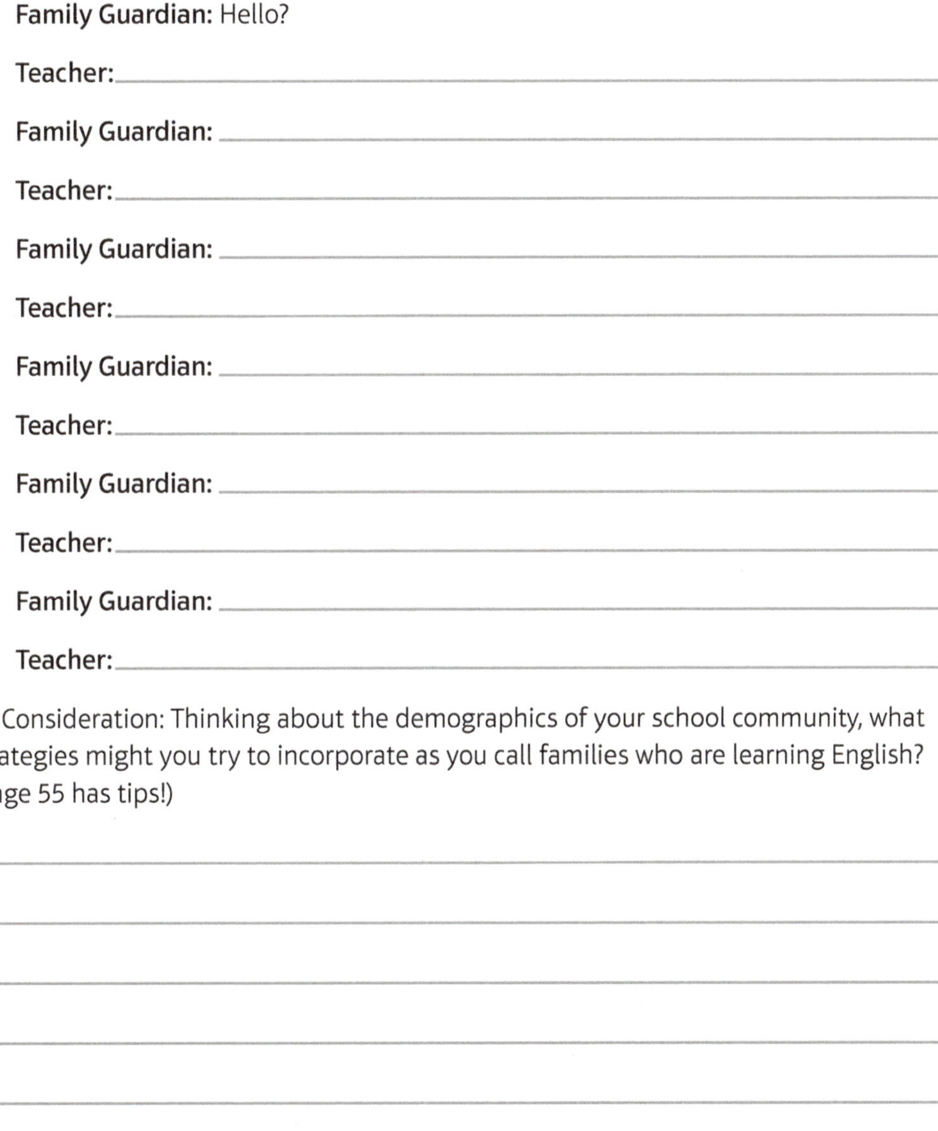

Family Guardian: Hello?

Teacher: ____________________

Family Guardian: ____________________

Teacher: ____________________

Family Guardian: ____________________

Teacher: ____________________

Family Guardian: ____________________

Teacher: ____________________

Family Guardian: ____________________

Teacher: ____________________

Family Guardian: ____________________

Teacher: ____________________

EL Consideration: Thinking about the demographics of your school community, what strategies might you try to incorporate as you call families who are learning English? (Page 55 has tips!)

____

____

____

____

____

____

TIP FOR VIRTUAL GROUPS

Welcome phone calls can be practiced virtually too! Participants can form partnerships and use an online messenger to type their script. Or better yet, participant pairs can practice their welcome call over the phone!

Foundational Strategy #2: Home Visits

Pages 56–65 discuss home visits extensively. While visits to your students' homes are undoubtedly more complicated than phone calls, as they need training, administrator support, prior planning, and dedicated time, they are also undeniably successful.

- If you have participated in a home visit before, choose one visit to reflect upon. How and why did it impact your relationship with the student and their family moving forward?
- If you have not yet participated in a home visit, choose two different students from past years of teaching and imagine how a home visit may have been able to change your relationship with them and their families. Record your thoughts below and be ready to share.

- If your school does not hold home visits, would you be comfortable advocating for them? Why or why not? If so, with whom in your school may you be able to address this? If possible, use this opportunity to discuss how home visits were initiated in your colleagues' school communities.

Foundational Strategy #3: An Invitation into the Classroom: Back-to-School Night and Open House

While it's easy to stick with what you've always done, this section discusses the potential impact these events can have if they're restructured to become more family focused.

Skim back through the suggestions on pages 66–70 about ways to make your family nights more hands-on. How could your restructure your next Back-to-School Night to ensure that family voices are included and amplified? How can you promote, in this event, that families are equal partners who can actively contribute?

Page 68 encourages every teacher to choose three key messages to present on Back-to-School Night—and even offers a few suggestions. No matter which messages you choose, the conversation should be kept as interactive as possible. If you were to think about all of the information that you normally relay on Back-to-School Night, how could you narrow it down to three key messages?

1.

2.

3.

Taking advantage of face-to-face opportunities in a meaningful manner is critical. Giving parents credit for their knowledge and important place in the process is so important. I loved a phrase in the book that called education a "team sport."

—PATRICIA JOMO, Freelancer in Family Engagement in Education, Greenwich Public Schools

EL Consideration: Watch the Chapter 3 Colleague Reflection video at www.scholastic.com/pro/PartnershipsResources.html. What strategies could you and your school try to incorporate into events like Back-to-School Night for families who are learning English? (Page 70 has a few tips!)

LOOKING BACK in order to LOOK AHEAD:

Always remember that you can engage in multiple ways...text, ClassDojo, email, phones, face-to-face. Our options are so large now.

—TERRI SCOTT, Family Engagement Coordinator for Title I Schools, NC

1 Out of everything you already do to initiate strong relationships with the families of the children you teach, which do you think are the most effective? Why?

2 Based on the strategies and ideas presented in this chapter, what can you commit to trying differently next school year?

Chapter 4: Transform Your Family Conferences and IEP Meetings

1a Think about the way *Powerful Partnerships* presents family conferences at the start of this chapter, and also consider how conferences are held in your classroom. Then use the rectangular Venn diagram below to analyze the similarities and differences between the two.

Key features of family conferences in *Powerful Partnerships*	Similarities	Key features of the conferences I hold

1b What are the two biggest differences between Dr. Mapp's family conference and the conferences you typically hold? What shift could you make to close that gap for each?

1. ______________________________

____

2. ______________________________

____

2 Pages 76–78 relay accounts of a variety of parent-teacher conferences. Which account(s) resonated with you? What qualities or characteristics would you like to include in your next round of conferences? Why?

____

____

3 Pages 82–83 acknowledge that sufficient time for family conferences is not always provided. When would you realistically be able to hold family conferences? What steps could you take to ensure that family conferences are held at this time?

____

____

TIP FOR FACILITATORS

- Use this halfway point as an opportunity to check in and ensure participants are benefiting from each session. Do group members have any suggestions for improvement?
- Ask participants to complete Questions 1a and 1b before meeting. Taking the time to reflect on the similarities between their own conferences and Dr. Mapp's family conferences will be a beneficial starting point as they plan for the future!

TIP FOR VIRTUAL GROUPS

Don't let the virtual nature of the group get in the way of personal shares. Ask participants in advance if anyone holds conferences similar to the ones Dr. Mapp presents. If you receive any positive responses, ask one or two educators to share their experience(s) with the group. How do they compare and contrast to Dr. Mapp's conferences? What key takeaways or tips can they share?

4 The second half of Chapter 4 focuses on Individualized Education Program (IEP) meetings. Dr. Mapp acknowledges that all teachers likely share one common characteristic: They have received little or no training on how to engage with families in the IEP process. She therefore presents strategies for the IEP process that revolve around two central ideas: Mind-set and Communication.

Keeping these strategies in mind, what are three actionable takeaways you gained from pages 83–100 regarding partnering with families during IEP meetings? Consider the backgrounds of your students' families and how you may apply the strategies on these pages to their unique needs.

Key takeaway	A personal goal statement to ensure I address this point next year	How will I know if I've achieved this goal?
1		
2		
3		

Throughout the year, our district has Family Newcomer Information Meetings. We present them in Spanish, French, and Arabic. We also try to translate important documents into those three languages.

—KELLY RALL, Hurst-Euless-Bedford ISD Coordinator of Family Engagement, Community Outreach, and Teacher Support

5a What do you already do to help families of students with an IEP? Based on what you have read, what else could you do to become an ally of your students' families throughout the IEP process?

5b What can you and your school do to make sure EL families feel welcome as well? (Page 99 provides recommendations, but tailor your answer to your own school community.)

LOOKING BACK in order to LOOK AHEAD:

1 Watch the Chapter 4 Colleague Reflection video at www.scholastic.com/pro/PartnershipsResources.html and listen to these educators reflect on what works well in their own family engagement. Then reflect: When you interact with families during meetings and conferences, what do you already do that you feel works well? What aspects of your meetings and conferences would you like to maintain next year?

2 Moving forward, how and when will you plan to share achievement data with your families, and how will you ensure that families also share their perspective on their child's progress?

3 Continuing to think about future parent meetings and conferences, how will you use the information in this chapter to help convey to families that they are the "experts" when it comes to knowing their children? In addition, how can you make sure you learn everything you can from families to help you best teach each child? Remember that no two families are alike and that you may need to use a variety of strategies to connect with all of the families in your classroom.

The Family Resource Center has an English for Families program where there are three components of the program: parent/child activity, parent language class, and child early learning playgroup. In addition, the parents have a WhatsApp group where they are sharing all sorts of information..."

—AMY YARBROUGH, Family Liaison, Family Resource Center, West Hartford, CT

WEEK SIX

Chapter 5: Maintain Strong Family Ties Throughout the Year

1 This chapter presents four case studies, so that you may use these examples to create a plan for maintaining your own strong family ties throughout the school year. Dr. Mapp, Ilene, and Jessica selected these case studies because they align with the five process conditions for planning successful family engagement events. By jotting a few notes in every square of the chart below, you will be able to visualize how each case study incorporates all five process conditions.

How are these process conditions present in the case studies below?	**CONDITION 1:** Directly linked to learning	**CONDITION 2:** Builds relationships between teachers and parents, and between parents	**CONDITION 3:** Collaborative, with equal participation and input from teachers, families, and students	**CONDITION 4:** Honors families' home languages, cultures, and experiences	**CONDITION 5:** Interactive, providing many and varied opportunities to learn together
We Are All History Makers: The Family Story Project					
Breaking Bread: A Case for Family Potlucks					
Global Connection: Building Partnerships w/ Immigrant Parents Through Texts					
Middle-School Passage Presentations					

2a What phrases or concepts appear often in your chart? Why do you think this is the case?

2b Are these themes common in your own classroom? Why or why not? If not, how could you incorporate them?

3a Of the four case studies presented, which one reminds you most of your own classroom? Why?

3b Are there any additional ideas from this case study that you could incorporate into what you already do? Consider changes that may help you connect with all of your students' families.

4a Of the four case studies presented, which one seems the farthest outside your comfort zone or the most different from anything you already do? Why do you think this case study struck you as the most unconventional?

4b The authors provide several reflection questions following each case study. Flip to the case study that you selected for #4a and thoughtfully consider the Reflect and Act questions provided in the chapter. Use the space below to jot down your answers and reactions to these questions.

TIP FOR FACILITATORS

- Encourage participants to review Question 1 before they read Chapter 5. They can then begin the chapter with a pencil in hand and complete the process condition chart as they read!
- Consider creating a group calendar that you can complete together as you discuss the *Looking Back in order to Look Ahead* section. Think about the best way to share the calendar once it's complete so participants have it as a resource moving forward. A shared online calendar or photocopies of what you create are two possibilities!

We have very positive feedback from parents when we combine Linked to Learning [Condition 1] with Interactive [Condition 5]. For example, we are now monitoring our own comprehension, so at our Parent Night we will invite parents and students, give them books that they can keep, and show everyone how to monitor their own comprehension. Then the parents do this with their child right then.

—KELLY RALL, Hurst-Euless-Bedford ISD Coordinator of Family Engagement, Community Outreach, and Teacher Support

TIP FOR VIRTUAL GROUPS

Create a space where all participants can list the opportunities they provide for families to participate in their children's learning, organized by month. This will create a robust calendar that all participants can refer back to throughout the school year!

As a regular classroom teacher, I always sent home a weekly progress note that became known as the "Blue Folder." This was one of the best ideas I adopted from my mentor during student teaching (18 years ago). It is a simple design with a three-check system for three categories and plenty of space for the parent to write back comments. Parents really appreciated seeing when their children did well and when something seemed off. They were also glad to write a short "happy note" about how they felt about their child.

—TERESA MATURINO RODRIGUEZ, Learning Strategies Classroom Teacher, Washington Elementary School, Manchester, CT

LOOKING BACK in order to LOOK AHEAD:

1 What opportunities do you provide for families to participate in their children's learning? To analyze how these opportunities progress throughout the year, record them in monthly increments below:

August, September, October: ____________________

November, December, January: ____________________

February, March, April: ____________________

May, June, July: ____________________

2 Examine the opportunities that you listed above and reflect on two factors:

Are there any points in the school year when there are not opportunities for families to engage in their children's learning? How can you fill these gaps with strategies presented in this chapter? Pages 115–117 as well as the Chapter 5 Colleague Reflection video (available at www.scholastic.com/pro/PartnershipsResources.html) may provide you with additional ideas.

Are there ample and varied opportunities for engagement with all families? Think especially about families who you may typically find more difficult to reach. What two or three strategies from this chapter could you employ over the next school year to reach these families?

1. ____________________

2. ____________________

3. ____________________

Chapter 6: Support Your Work with Family-Friendly Resources

1 Up to this point, you have focused on what you can do to build meaningful relationships with your students' families. This chapter, however, acknowledges that *you can't do it all. You need help and support in order to be successful!*

As you look toward next school year and the important work you hope to accomplish, what alliances do you already have that you know you can depend on? What additional alliances might be beneficial for you to form? Consider individuals and organizations that can support you both professionally and personally.

2 This chapter also discusses self-care and the importance of taking the time to focus on your own well-being. You need to be at your own personal best before you are capable of truly helping others. What have you done in the past that helps you feel healthy and happy? What is something you can commit to doing regularly to continue this positivity and self-care throughout the year?

3 Pages 122–129 provide a variety of templates and tools that you can use as you move forward in building strong partnerships. Make note of a few below that you think would be the most helpful to you. Recording them here now may help you remember them later when you need them most!

TIP FOR FACILITATORS

- Challenge participants to use Question 4's template to create a draft of their welcome letter before meeting. Part of this book study session can then be used to share their letters and receive constructive feedback from their peers.
- Ask participants, if they are able, to bring a device with internet access to this session. Much of this chapter focuses on online resources, and having devices will enable participants to investigate these resources with each other.

What's going to be the foundation for success for the whole rest of the year is building that relationship and staying in regular touch.

—ANNE HENDERSON, Co-author of *Beyond the Bake Sale: The Essential Guide to Family-School Partnerships*

4 Page 126 introduces the concept of a welcome letter, which can be distributed to families at the beginning of the school year in order to introduce yourself, share your contact information, and underscore the importance of family/teacher partnerships. Use the template below to draft your own welcome letter. The goal is that your completed draft will serve as a resource that you can refer to and tweak for years to come!

____

Date

______________________________,

Friendly Greeting

Quick welcome:

____

____

Background about yourself and your educational philosophy:

____

____

Information about how you will stay in touch and work to build strong family partnerships throughout the year:

____

____

Brief curricular overview/what to expect this school year:

____

____

Wrap-up and any important closing information, including contact information if not shared already:

____

____

Friendly closing and signature:

____

____

LOOKING BACK in order to LOOK AHEAD:

TIP FOR VIRTUAL GROUPS

Since you have the benefit of already being online, you can easily share actual website links with each other. Provide time for participants to explore website resources that the book and other participants share.

1 Pages 129–139 provide a lengthy list of additional resources, including organizations, professional development opportunities, books and articles, classroom resources, and evaluation tools. While it can be easy to skim through this list, take the time to truly read these pages.

Then choose at least one resource that you think would have been helpful over the last school year. If it would have come in handy in the past, it will likely be helpful in the future as well! Once you have selected a resource, use the website provided to investigate it. Then record at least a couple important takeaways in the space below:

2 It's hard to anticipate what next year may bring, and only you can predict what may be helpful as you tackle a new year of creating strong family partnerships. As you try to form meaningful partnerships with every family in your class, no matter their background, what are three resources from the list provided that may prove beneficial to you? Record them below, along with a note of why you chose them so you can quickly refer to this when you need assistance in the future!

1. ______

2. ______

3. ______

WEEK EIGHT

Brainstorming for the Future

From examining your own core beliefs to learning about the power of partnerships and exploring how to build strong relationships with your students' families, you have covered a lot of ground over the course of this book study! Unlike the preceding chapters, this final reflection will not align to a specific chapter; rather, it is designed to help you consider the *Powerful Partnerships* book as a whole in order to build an action plan for moving forward.

Before you complete the action plan below, make sure you have your book and your completed book study pages easily accessible. You are about to put everything together and create a tangible plan to help guide you through the year(s) ahead!

TIP FOR FACILITATORS

- Remind participants that this will be the final session, and encourage them to share lingering questions in advance so you make sure to address them!
- This last session could be a beneficial time to invite a guest speaker. Do you know a professional outside your group who specializes in family engagement? Or perhaps a parent who would enjoy sharing his/her experiences? Your group may have suggestions as well.
- Prepare to send a final email summarizing your time together. You may want to share participant contact information and/or include a follow-up survey to evaluate the book study.

1 **Revisit Your Goals** Flip back to the Looking Ahead section of the Action Guide's Introduction. In the very last question, you considered the aspects of family engagement in your classroom that you hoped to grow and improve. Reread your goal statement, and then consider what you've learned over the course of this book study.

Do you feel better equipped to achieve this goal now that your reading is complete? Why or why not? If not, what else could you do to make sure your goal is achievable?

Considering the engagement strategies that you have learned, are there any additional goals you hope to achieve regarding family partnerships in your classroom? Think about what you can do to not only reach every student's family but to also create a lasting partnership with them. Then record your new goal(s) here.

2 Develop a Plan Without a plan, a goal is just a goal. A goal only has the potential to become a success story when a plan is in place. While the concepts and strategies presented in *Powerful Partnerships* are still fresh in your mind, use the action plan template on the following pages to map out the year ahead. The template has been designed to break down the school year into key increments so you can consider how to build, create, and maintain powerful partnerships with each of your student's families over the course of the entire school year.

TIP FOR VIRTUAL GROUPS

If your meetings have been more chat-centered, this last meeting could be a great opportunity to "meet" face-to-face! There are many online forums that cater to group video chats, and a quick web search should help you find one that best fits your needs.

MY ACTION PLAN FOR FAMILY ENGAGEMENT

Timing	Partnership and engagement strategies I will employ:	Steps I will take to make sure I successfully complete these strategies:	How I will engage all families, including those who speak another language, seem more difficult to reach, etc.:
What will I do before the school year begins?	*Consider: Welcome phone calls, home visits, and welcome letters*		
What will I do at the beginning of the school year?	*Consider: Messaging at Back-to-School Night/ Open House, including ice breakers, scavenger hunts, "Hopes and Dreams" letters, and opportunities for parent interaction*		
What will I do throughout the school year?	*Consider: How you will consistently involve parents as equal partners, maintain ongoing positive communication, and engage families in the learning*		
What will I do at the end of the school year?	*Consider: End-of-year celebrations, parent surveys, moving up events, etc.*		

TIP FOR VIRTUAL GROUPS

Before you close the discussion forum, consider where your virtual sessions can continue to live. This will enable the information you discussed to serve as an ongoing resource throughout the school year.

What's most important is to begin the work and do something. If you've read the Powerful Partnerships *book and you know there is a whole year's worth of family engagement practices that can be done to create the strongest family engagement possible, don't let that be an intimidating factor. What's really important is to begin the work. Build your practice from there.*

—ILENE CARVER, Co-author of *Powerful Partnerships*

If I need help with any part of my action plan, I can reach out to:
(Consider colleagues, school stakeholders, professional organizations, etc.)

3 Persevere Always remember that the process of building and maintaining relationships with your students' families is an ongoing commitment. You may have the best-laid plans only to turn them all upside down when they don't seem to be working. As you refer to your action plan throughout the school year, don't be afraid to add, cross out, erase, and start over. With resilience and dedication, as well as an open mind and a fervent belief that all families want to be engaged in their child's learning, you are bound to achieve powerful family partnerships!